THE USBORNE
FIRST THOUSAND WORDS
IN ARABIC

Heather Amery
Illustrated by Stephen Cartwright

Revised edition by Mairi Mackinnon and Edward Bond
Picture editing by Mike Olley
Arabic language consultants:
Nader Ibrahim and Fatima Merheb Dabboussi

There is a little yellow duck to find on every double page. Can you find it?

Stephen Cartwright's
little yellow duck made
his first-ever appearance in *The First
Thousand Words* over thirty years ago.
Duck has since featured in over 125
titles, in more than 70 languages, and
has delighted millions of readers,
both young and old,
around the world.

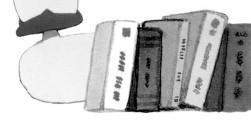

This revised edition first published in 2014 by Usborne Publishing Ltd, 83-85 Saffron Hill, London EC1N 8RT. www.usborne.com
Based on a previous title first published in 1979. Copyright © 2014, 1995, 1979 Usborne Publishing Ltd.

About this book

The First Thousand Words in Arabic is an enormously popular book that has helped many thousands of children and adults learn new words and improve their Arabic language skills.

You'll find it easy to learn words by looking at the **small labelled pictures**. Then you can practise the words by talking about the large central pictures. There is a guide under each Arabic word, showing you how to pronounce it. You can also **hear the words** on the Usborne Quicklinks website: just go to **www.usborne.com/ quicklinks** and enter the keywords **1000 arabic**. There you can find links to other useful websites about the Arabic language and Arabic-speaking countries.

There is a **word list** at the back of the book, which you can use to look up words in the picture pages.

Remember, this is a book of a thousand words. It will take time to learn them all.

The Arabic language
Arabic is the language of the Koran or Qur'an, and is the official language of 22 countries, from Morocco to Iraq. Over such a huge area, everyday spoken Arabic can be very different from one country to another. A version called Modern Standard Arabic is widely used for formal speech and writing, including newspapers, radio and television. The words in this book are in Modern Standard Arabic.

Reading and writing Arabic
There are some important differences between the written forms of Arabic and English. As you can see here, **Arabic has its own alphabet**. On page 56 of this book you will find a guide to the alphabet, telling you how to pronounce each letter.

Unlike English, **Arabic is read from right to left**. (The pronunciation guides in this book should still be read from left to right, as though they were English words.)

When you look at the Arabic words in this book, you will also notice extra dashes and other marks above and below the letters. These are used to show short vowel sounds and long consonants. Normally, Arabic is written without these signs, but books for beginners and children will include them.

The pronunciation guides have been made as simple as possible: in general, you just say what you see.

ألوان
alwaan

زُجاجات
zujaajaat

سَمَك ذَهَبِي
samak thahabee

طائِرة مروحيّة
taa'ira mirwahiyya

لُعبة تركيبيّة
lu'ba tarkeebiyya

شوكولاتة
shokolaata

الـمَنزِل
al-manzil

مَغطَس
maghtas

صابون
saaboon

صُنبور
sunboor

وَرَق حَمام
waraq hammaam

فُرشاة أسنان
furshaat asnaan

ماء
maa'

مِرحاض
mirhaad

ليفة
leefah

مَغسَلة
maghsala

مِرشّة
mirashah

منشَفة
minshafa

4

حَمّام
hammaam

غُرفة جُلوس
ghurfat julus

سَرير
sareer

مَعجون أسنان
ma'joon asnaan

مِذياع
mizyaa'

مخَدّة
mikhadda

قُرص مُدمَج
qurs modmaj

سَجّادة
sajjaada

أريكة
areeka

كُرسي
kursee

لِحاف
lihaaf

مِشط
misht

شَرشَف
sharshaf

حَصيرة
haseera

خَزانة
khazaana

تِلفزيون
telefiziyoun

صُوان
sowan

مِرآة
mir'aa

فُرشاة شعر
furshaat sha'r

مِصباح
misbaah

مُلصَقات
mulsaqaat

عَلاقة
'allaaqa

هاتِف
haatif

دَرَج
daraj

غُرفة نوم
ghurfat nawm

مَدخَل
madkhal

جِهاز تَدفِئَة
jihaz tadfiaah

فواكِه
fawaakih

جَريدة
jareeda

طاوِلة
taawila

رَسائل
rasaa'il

المَطبَخ al-matbakh

ثَلاجة
thallaaja

أكواب
akwaab

ساعة حائط
saa'at ha'it

كُرسي
kursee

مَلاعق صغيرة
malaa'iq sagheera

مِفتاح الكَهرَباء
miftaah ul-kahrabaa'

مَسحوق غَسيل
mashooq ghaseel

مِفتاح
miftaah

باب
baab

مكنسة كَهرَبائية
miknasa kahrabaa'iya

حَوض الجلي
hawd ul-jalee

طَناجِر
tanaajir

شُوَك
shuwak

مِريلة
miryala

طاولة الكي
taawilat ul-kay

زِبالة
zibaala

6

إبريق شاي
ibreek shaay

سَكاكين
sakaakeen

مِمسَحة بِعَصا
mimsaha bi'asaa

مِمسَحة
mimsaha

بَلاط
balaat

مكنسة
miknasá

غَسالة
ghasaala

مَجرود
majrood

دُرج
durj

صُحون صغيرة
suhoon sagheera

مقلاة
miqlaa

فُرن
furn

مَلاعِق خَشَب
malaa'iq khashab

صُحون
suhoon

مكواة
mikwaa

خَزانة حائط
khazaanat haa'it

فوطة
foota

فَناجين
fanaajeen

عُلبة كبريت
'ulbat kibreet

فُرشاة
furshaa

طاسات
taasaat

7

البُستان al-bustaan

مِرَّش
mirrash

عَرَبة يد
'arabat yad

خَلية نحل
khaliyat nahl

حَلَزون
halazoon

طوب
toob

حَمامة
hamaama

مِجرَفة
mijrafa

دُعسوقة
du'sooqa

زبالة
zibaala

بُذور
budhoor

مَخزَن
makhzan

دودة أرض
doodat ard

أزهار
azhaar

رَشاش ماء
rashaash maa'

مِجرَفة
mijrafa

دَبّور
dabboor

نَحلة
nahla

مَسطَرين
mastareen

عَظمة
'athma

سِياج
siyaaj

شوكة
shawka

مقَص الحَشيش
miqass ul-hasheesh

مَمر
mamarr

أوراق شجَر
awraaq shajar

شَجَرة
shajara

دُخان
dukhaan

دودة
dooda

مِشط زراعي
misht zira'ee

عُش
'ush

غصون
ghusoon

أعشاب
aa'shaab

عَرَبة أطفال
'arabat atfaal

خُضروات
khudrawaat

نار
naar

خُرطوم
khurtoom

بيت بلاستيك
bayt plaasteek

9

الوَرشة

al-warsha

بَراغي صغيرة
baraaghee sagheera

مَلزَمة
malzama

وَرَق زُجاج
waraq zujaaj

المِثقَب
al-mithqab

سُلَّم
sullam

مِنشار
minshaar

نِشارة
nishaara

تَقويم
taqweem

صُندوق الأدوات
sundooq ul-adwaat

مفَك
mifak

لوح خَشَب
lawh khashab

نِجارة
nijaara

مطواة
matwaa

مَسامير رَسم
masaameer rasim

عنكبوت
'ankaboot

بَراغي
baraaghee

عَزقات
'azakaat

نسيج عنكبوت
naseej 'ankaboot

بَرميل
barmeel

ذُبابة
thubaaba

فَأس
fa's

مِتر
mitr

مِطرَقة
mitraqa

مَبرد
mabrad

عُلبة دِهان
'ulbat dihaan

قطع خَشَب
qita' khashab

مَسامير
masaameer

طاولة نجارة
taawilat nijaara

مَرطَبانات
martabaanaat

فارة
faara

11

الشارِع ash-shaari'

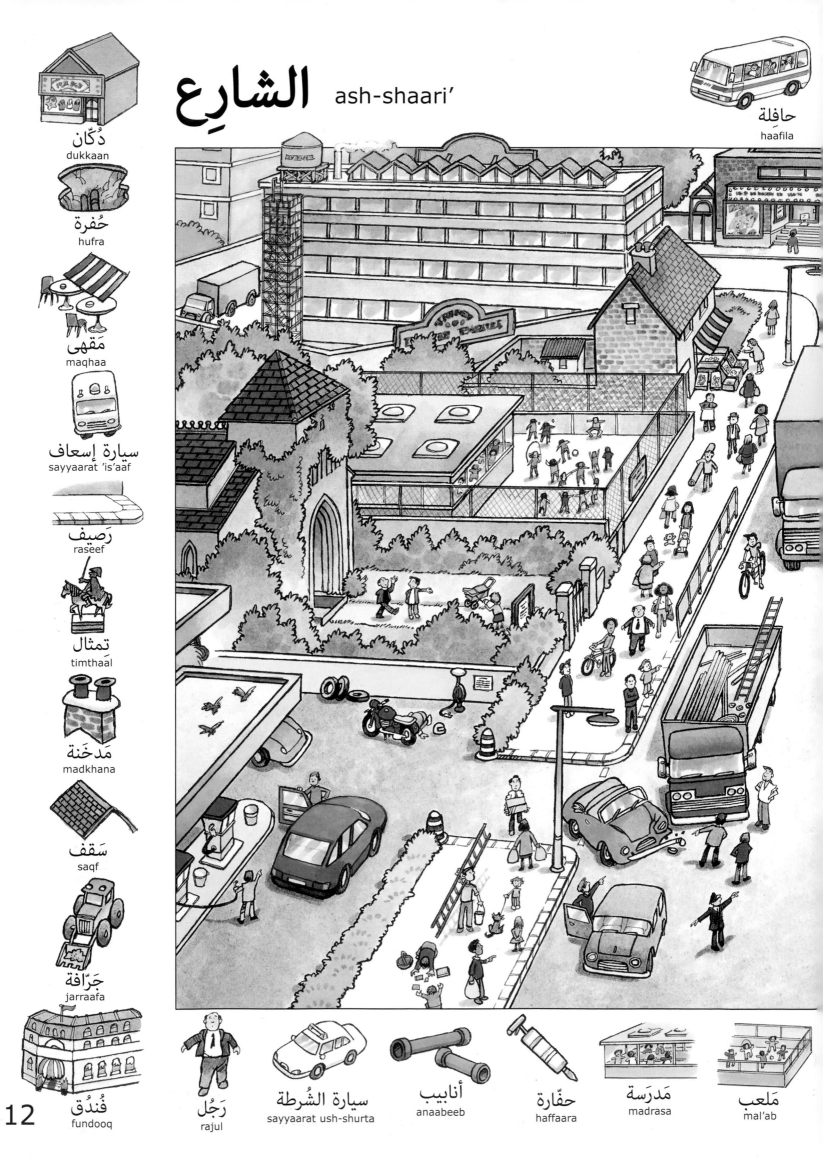

دُكّان
dukkaan

حُفرة
hufra

مَقهى
maqhaa

سيارة إسعاف
sayyaarat 'is'aaf

رَصيف
raseef

تمثال
timthaal

مَدخَنة
madkhana

سَقف
saqf

جَرّافة
jarraafa

حافِلة
haafila

12

فُندُق
fundooq

رَجُل
rajul

سيارة الشُرطة
sayyaarat ush-shurta

أنابيب
anaabeeb

حفّارة
haffaara

مَدرَسة
madrasa

مَلعب
mal'ab

سيّارة أُجرة
sayyaarat ujra

مَمر مُشاة
mamarr mushaa

مَصنع
masna'

شاحِنة
shaahina

إشارات ضوئية
ishaaraat dawiya

دار السينما
dar us-seenima

سيّارة شَحن
sayyaarat shahn

مِحدَلة
mihdala

عَرَبة
'araba

دار
daar

سوق
sooq

أدراج
adraaj

دَرّاجة نارية
darraaja naariya

شُقق
shooqaq

دَرّاجة
darraaja

سيّارة الإطفاء
sayyaarat ul-'itfaa'

شُرطي
shurtee

سيّارة
sayyaara

إمرأة
'imra'a

عَمود إنارة
'amood inara'

13

دُكّان الألعاب
dukkaan ul-al'aab

قِطار كَهرِبائي
qitaar kahrabaa'ee

زَهر
zahr

مِزمار
mizmaar

إنسان آلي
insaan aalee

طَوق
tawq

آلة تصوير
aalat tasweer

خَرَز
kharaz

دُمى
dumaa

جيتار
geetar

خاتِم
khaatim

دار دُمى
dar dumaa

هارمونيكا
harmoonikaa

صَفّارة
saffara

مُكَعَبات
muka'abaat

قلعة
qal'a

غَوّاصة
ghawwaasa

بوق
booq

سِهام
sihaam

14

قوس
qaws

مِظَلَة
mithalla

مركِب شراعي
markib shiraa'ee

دهان الوجه
dihaan-ul-wajh

محدَلة
mihdala

أقنعة
aqni'a

سيارة سِباق
sayyaarat sibaaq

حِصان هزاز
hisaan hazzaz

حَصّالة
hassaala

غُلَل
ghulal

عرائس
'araa'is

بيانو
piyanoo

روّاد فضاء
ruwwaad fadaa'

رافِعة
raafi'a

أوراق اللَعِب
awraaq al-la'ab

طبول
tubool

جنود دُمى
junood dumaa

صُندوق ألوان
sundooq alwaan

صاروخ
saarookh

15

الحَديقة العامة

al-hadeeqat
ul-ʼaamma

مَقعد
maqʼad

أُرجوحة
orjooha

حوض رَمل
hawd raml

نُزهة
nuzha

طيّارة وَرَق
tayyaarat
waraq

بوظة
bootha

كَلب
kalb

بوابة
bawwaaba

طَريق
tareeq

ضفدع
difdaʼ

زُحلوقة
zuhlooqa

16

فِراخ ضِفدع
firakhu difdaʼ

بُحيرة
buhaira

أحذية تَزلُّج
ahthiyat tazalluj

شجيرة
shujayra

رَضيع
radee'

لَوحة تَزَلُّج
lawhat tazalluj

تُراب
turaab

عَرَبة أطفال
'arabat atfaal

ميزان
meezaan

أطفال
atfaal

دَرّاجة ثُلاثية
darraaja thulaathiya

عَصافير
'asaafeer

سِياج
siyaaj

كُرة
kura

قارِب
qaarib

خيط
khait

بُرَيْكة
burayka

فِراخ بط
firakhu batt

حَبل القَفز
habl al-qafz

شَجَر
shajar

حَوض زَرع
hawdu zar'

بَجَعة
baja'a

رَسَن
rasan

بطة
batta

17

الحَيَوانات
al-hayawaanaat

جَناح
janaah

صَقر
saqr

فرس البحر
faras ul-bahr

بندة
panda

كُفوف
kufoof

كنغر
kangar

خَفّاش
khaffaash

غوريلا
ghooreela

قِرد
qird

صَخرة جليد
sakhrat jaleed

ذَيْل
thayl

ذئب
th'ib

بَطريق
batreeq

تِمساح
timsaah

دُبّ
dubb

ريش
reesh

بَجَعة
baja'a

نَعامة
na'aama

دُلفين
dolfeen

زَرافة
zaraafa

أَسَد
asad

أشبال
ashbaal

أيل
ayl

جَمَل
jamal

فَقَمة
faqma

دُبّ قُطبي
dub qutbee

سُلحفاة
sulhafaa

خَرطوم
khartoom

فيل
feel

كَركَدَن
karkadan

ثور أمريكي
thawr amreekee

قَرن
qarn

سَمّور
sammoor

ماعِز
maa'iz

حِمار وَحشي
himaar wahshee

حية
hayya

سَمَك قِرش
samak qirsh

حوت
hoot

نَمِر
namir

فَهد
fahd

19

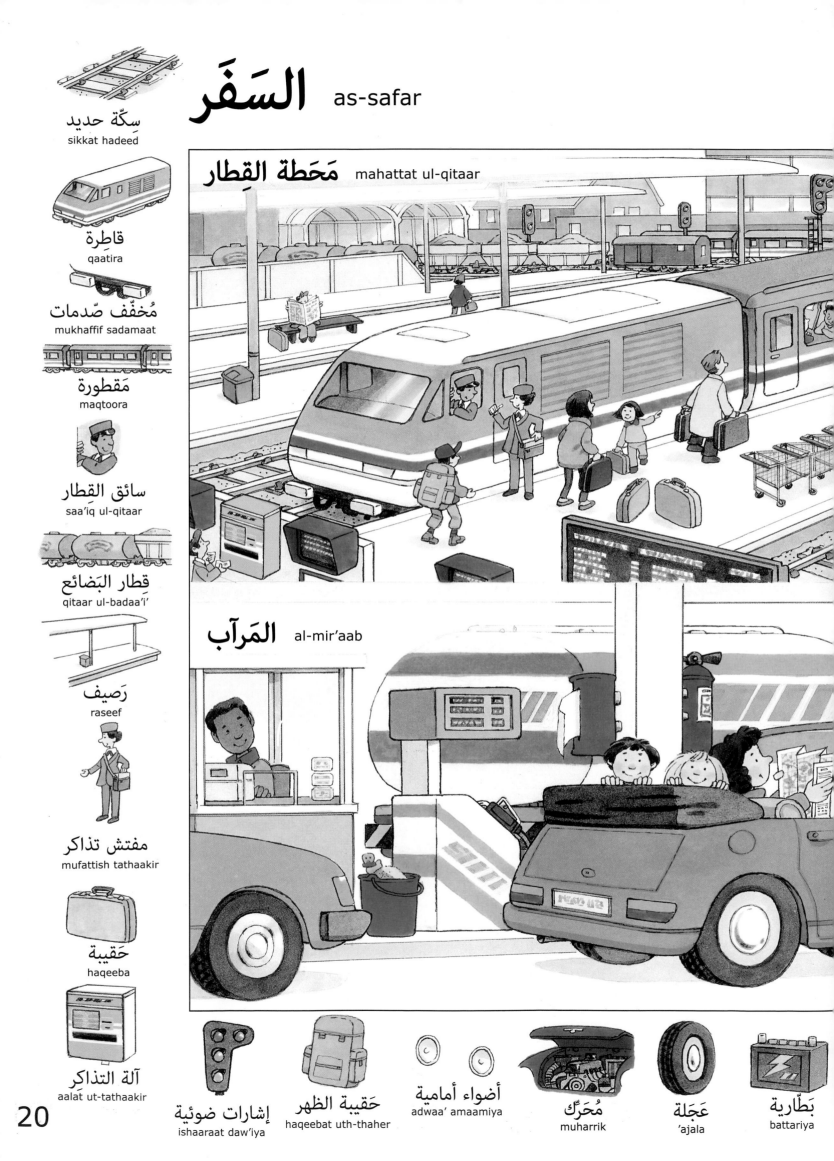

السَفَر as-safar

سِكّة حديد
sikkat hadeed

قاطِرة
qaatira

مُخفّف صّدمات
mukhaffif sadamaat

مَقطورة
maqtoora

سائق القِطار
saa'iq ul-qitaar

قِطار البَضائع
qitaar ul-badaa'i'

رَصيف
raseef

مفتش تذاكِر
mufattish tathaakir

حَقيبة
haqeeba

آلة التذاكِر
aalat ut-tathaakir

20

مَحَطة القِطار mahattat ul-qitaar

المَرآب al-mir'aab

إشارات ضوئية
ishaaraat daw'iya

حَقيبة الظهر
haqeebat uth-thaher

أضواء أمامية
adwaa' amaamiya

مُحَرّك
muharrik

عَجَلة
'ajala

بَطّارية
battariya

طائرة
taa'ira

طائِرة مروحيّة
taa'ira mirwahiyya

مُدَرَّج
mudarraj

بُرج المُراقَبة
burj ul-muraaqaba

المَطار   al-mataar

طاقَم الطائرة
taakam-ut-taa'ira

طيار
tayyaar

مَغْسل سيارات
maghsal sayyaarat

صُندوق
sundooq

بَنزين
banzeen

سيارة تصليح
sayyaarat tasleeh

مَغسَلة سيارات

مَضَخَّة البنزين
madakha al-banzeen

شاحِنة نفط
shaahinat nift

مِفتاح
miftaah

دولاب
doolaab

غِطاء المُحَرِّك
ghitaa' ul-muharrik

زيت
zayt

21

دولاب هواء
doolaab hawa'

مِنطاد
mintaad

فَراشة
faraasha

سِحليّة
sihliyya

حِجارة
hijaara

ثَعلب
tha'lab

جَدوَل
jadwal

عَمود الاتجاهات
'amood ul-itijaahat

قُنفُذ
qunfuth

سَدّ
sadd

الريف ar-reef

جَبَل
jabal

سِنجاب
sinjaab

غابة
ghaaba

غُرَيَر
ghurayir

نَهر
nahr

طَريق
tareeq

خِيام
khiyaam

قَناة
qanaa

جذوع الشَجر
juthoo' ush-shajar

قَرية
qariya

فَراشة ليل
faraashat layl

جِسر
jisr

مَركَب بَضائع
markab badaa'i'

شَلال
shallaal

بومة
booma

نَفق
nafaq

جِراء ثعلب
jiraa' tha'lab

خُلد
khuld

صيّاد سمَك
sayyaad samak

صُخور
sukhoor

عَلجوم
'aljoom

قِطار
qitaar

بيت مُتنقّل
bayt mutanakkel

تَلّ
tal

23

مَتبَنة
matbana

كَلب الراعي
kalb ur-raa'ee

غَنَم
ghanam

بِركة
birka

صيصان
seesaan

مَخزَن القَمح
makhzan ul-qamh

حَظيرة الخَنازير
hatheerat ul-khanaazeer

ثور
thawr

قُن دَجاج
qun dajaaj

المَزرَعة al-mazra'a

ديك
deek

عَرَبة
'araba

جَرّار
jarrar

إوزّ
iwazz

شاحِنة صهريج
shaahinat sahreej

حَظيرة
hatheera

وَحل
wahl

عَرَبة
'araba

24

مُزارِع
muzaari'

حَقِل
haql

دَجاج
dajaaj

عِجل
'ijl

سِياج
siyaaj

سَرج
sarj

حَظيرة بَقر
hatheerat baqar

بَقرة
baqara

مِحراث
mihraath

بُستان فاكِهة
bustaan faakiha

إسطَبل
istabl

خَنانيص
khanaanees

حِمار
himaar

ديوك حَبَش
duyook habash

فَزاعة
fazaa'a

مَزرعة
mazra'a

تِبن
tibn

خِرفان
khirfaan

حُزَم التِبن
huzam at-tibn

حِصّان
hissaan

خَنازير
khanaazeer

25

شاطىء البَحر shaati' al-bahr

مرْكِب شراعي
markib shiraa'ee

صَدَفة
sadafa

بَحر
bahr

مِجداف
mijdaaf

مَنارة
manara

مِجرَفة
mijrafa

سَطل
satl

نَجمةالبَحر
najmat ul-bahr

قَلعة رَمْلية
qala'a ramliya

شمَسية
shamsiya

عَلم
'alam

بَحّار
bahhaar

سَرطان
sarataan

نورَس
nawras

جَزيرة
jazeera

قارب سريع
qaarib saree'

تزَلُّج مائي
tazalluj maa'ee

26

أمواج
amwaaj

قُبّعة القَش
qubba'at ul-qash

جُرف
jurf

سَفينة
safeena

زَورَق
zawraq

حَبل
habl

حَصى
hasaa

طَحالِب
tahaaleb

شَبَكة
shabaka

مِجداف
mijdaaf

قارب صيد
qaarib sayd

زَعانِف
za'aanif

واقي شَمسي
waaqee shamsee

سَمَك
samak

ملابس السباحة
malaabis us-sibaaha

ناقلة نَفط
naaqilat naft

شاطىء
shaati'

زَورَق
zawraq

كُرسي مَرکَب
kursee markab

27

المَدرَسة al-madrasa

مِقَصّ
miqass

٢ + ٢ = ٤
٣ + ٢ = ٥

حِساب
hisaab

مِمحاة
mimhaa

مِسطَرة
mistara

صُوَر
suwar

أقلام لَبّاد
aqlaam labbad

طين للتَشكيل
teen lit-tashkeel

ألوان
alwaan

وَلَد
walad

قلم رصاص
qalm rasaas

مَكتَب
maktab

كُتُب
kutub

قَلَم حِبر
qalam hibr

غِراء
ghiraa'

طَباشير
tabaasheer

رَسم
rasm

لوح
lawh

سَلة المُهمَلات
sallat ul-muhmalaat

أُستاذة
ustaatha

صُندوق
sundooq

خَريطة
khareeta

ريشة
reesha

سَقف
saqf

حائط
haa'it

أرضية
ardiyya

دَفتَر
daftar

الحروف الأبجدية
al-huroof al-abjadiyya

شارة
shaara

حوض سَمَك
hawd samak

وَرَق
waraq

ستار
sitaar

أ ب ت ث ج ح خ د ذ ر ز
س ش ص ض ط ظ ع غ ف
ق ك ل م ن ة ه و ي

مقبض الباب
mikbad ul-bab

نَبتة
nabta

كُرة أرضية
kura ardiyya

بِنت
bint

ألوان شَمع
alwaan sham'

مِصباح
misbaah

لوح أسود
lawh aswad

29

مُمَرِّض
mumarrid

قُطن
qutn

دَواء
dawaa'

مِصعَد
mis'ad

رِداء
ridaa'

عُكّازات
'ukkazaat

أقراص دَواء
aqraas dawaa'

صينية
seeniya

ساعة يد
saa'at yad

ميزان حَرارة
meezaan haraara

سِتار
sitaar

الْمُسْتَشْفى al-mustashfaa

تُفّاحة
tuffaaha

جِبس
jibs

ضَماد
dimaad

كُرسي متحرك
kursee mutaharrek

لُعبة تركيبية
lu'ba tarkeebiyya

طبيبة
tabeeba

مِحْقَنة
mihqana

الطَبيب
at-tabeeb

نعال
ni'aal

حاسوب
hasoob

ضِماد لاصِق
dimaad laasiq

موز
mawz

عِنَب
'inab

سَلّة
salla

أَلعاب
al'aab

إجّاص
ijjaas

بطاقات
bitaaqaat

حِفاض
hifaad

عصا
'asaa

وسادة
wisaada

قَميص نوم
qamees nawm

لِباس نوم
libaas nawm

بُرتُقالة
burtuqaala

مَناديل وَرق
manaadeel waraq

مجَلّة فُكاهية
majalla fukahiyya

قاعة الانتظار
qaa'at ul-intithaar

31

الحَفلة al-hafla

هَدايا
hadaaya

بالُون
baaloon

شوكولاتة
shokolaata

نَظارات
nathaaraat

حَلْوى
halwaa

نافذة
naafitha

ألعاب نارية
al'aab naariya

شَريطة
shareeta

كَعكة
ka'ka

مصاصة الشرب
massasat ush-shurb

شَمعَة
sham'a

ورق زينة
waraq zeena

ألعاب
al'aab

32

يوسفي
yusufee

سُجُق
sujuq

دُب
dub

نَقانِق
naqaaniq

شرائح البطاطا
sharaa'ih ul-bataata

أزياء تَنَكُّرية
azyaa' tanakkuriya

گَرَز
karaz

عَصير فَواكه
'aseer fawaakih

توت
toot

فَراوَلة
faraawala

مِصباح
misbaah

شَطيرة
shateera

زُبدة
zubda

بَسكوت
baskoot

جُبنة
jubna

خُبز
khubz

غطاء المائدة
ghitaa' ul-maa'ida

33

البِقالة al-biqaala

خضر و فواكه

جبنة

غرِيبفروت graybfroot

جَزَر jazar

قُنَّبيط qunnabeet

كُراث kuraath

فِطر fitr

خِيار khiyaar

ليمون laymoon

كَرَفس karafs

مِشمِش mishmish

شمّام shammaam

34

أكياس akyaas

بَصَل basal

مَلفوف malfoof

دُراق durraq

خَس khass

بازلاء bazillaa'

بَندورة banadoora

بيض
bayd

خَوخ
khawkh

طَحين
taheen

ميزان
meezaan

مَرطَبانات
martabaanaat

لَحم
lahm

أناناس
anaanaas

لَبَن رائب
laban raa'ib

سَلّة
salla

زُجاجات
zujaajaat

حَقيبة يد
haqeebat yad

محفَظة
mihfaza

نقود
nuqood

مُعلَّبات
mu'allabaat

عَرَبة
'araba

بَطاطا
bataata

سَبانِخ
sabaanikh

فاصولياء
fasooliyaa'

صُندوق الدَفع
sundooq ad-daf'

قرع
qar'

35

الأكل   al-akl

فُطور
futoor

غَداء
ghadaa'

بيض مَسلوق
bayd maslooq

قَهوة
qahwa

بيض مقلي
bayd maqlee

خُبز مُحَمَّص
khubz muhammas

مُرَبّى
murabbaa

قشدة
qishda

حَليب
haleeb

رقائق الحبوب
raqa'iq ul-huboob

شوكولاتة ساخنة
shokolaata saakhina

سُكَّر
sukkar

شاي
shaay

عَسَل
'asal

مِلح
milh

فِلفِل
filfil

إبريق شاي
ibreek shaay

فطائر
fataa'ir

أقراص خُبز
aqraas khubz

36

عَشاء
ashaa'

لَحم
lahm

حَساء
hasaa'

عُجّة
'ujja

سَلَطة
salata

عِصي
'isee

بُرغُر
burger

دَجاج
dajaaj

أُرُز
aruz

صلصة بَندورة
salsat banadoora

مَعكَرونة
ma'karoona

بَطاطا مَهروسة
bataata mahroosa

بِتزة
bitza

بطاطا مَقلية
bataata maqliyya

حلوِيّات
halwiyyaat

أنا ana

رأس
ra's

شَعر
sh'ar

وَجه
wajh

ذِراع
thiraa'

كوع
koo'

بَطن
batn

أصابِع القَدَم
asaabi' al-qadam

قَدَم
qadam

رِجل
rijl

رُكبة
rukba

حاجِب
haajib

عَين
'ayn

أنف
anf

خَدّ
khadd

فَم
fam

شِفاه
shifaah

أسنان
asnaan

لِسان
lisaan

ذَقن
thaqn

آذان
aathaan

رَقَبة
raqaba

أكْتاف
aktaaf

صَدر
sadr

ظَهر
thahr

مُؤخّرة
mu'akhira

يَد
yad

إبهام
ibhaam

أصابِع
asaabi'

مَلابِسي malaabisee

جوارِب
jawaarib

سِروال داخلي
sirwaal daakhilee

قَميص داخلي
qamees daakhilee

سِروال
sirwaal

جينز
jeens

قَميص
qamees

تَنّورة
tannoora

قَميص
qamees

رَبطة عنق
rabtat 'unuq

سِروال قَصير
sirwaal qaseer

جَورب طويل
jawrab taweel

فُستان
fustaan

كَنزة صوف
kanzat soof

قَميص
qamees

سُترة صوف
sutrat soof

شال
shaal

مِنديل
mindeel

حِذاء رياضي
hithaa' riyaadee

حِذاء
hithaa'

صندل
sandal

جَزمة
jazma

قفازان
quffaazaan

حِزام
hizaam

إبزيم
ibzeem

سَحّاب
sahhaab

رباط
ribaat

زِرّ
zirr

عُروة
'urwa

جيوب
juyoob

معطَف
mi'taf

سُترة
sutra

طاقية
taaqiya

قُبّعة
qubba'a

39

الناس
an-naas

طَبّاخ
tabbaakh

راقِص
raaqis

راقِصة
raaqisa

مُمَثّل
mumathil

مُمَثّلة
mumathila

مُغَنّي
mughani

مُغَنّية
mughaniya

رائد فَضاء
raa'id fadaa'

لَحّام
lahhaam

الشُرطي
ash-shurtee

الشُرطية
ash-shurtiya

نَجّار
najjaar

رَجُل إطفاء
rajul itfaa'

فَنّانة
fannaana

قاضٍ
qaadin

ميكانيكي
meekaaneekee

ميكانيكية
mikaaneekiya

40

حَلّاق
hallaaq

سائقة شاحنة
saaiqat shaahina

سائق حافلة
saa'iq haafila

طَبيبة أسنان
tabeebat asnaan

غَوّاص
ghawaas

نادل
naadil

نادلة
naadila

ساعي البريد
saa'i-l bareed

دَهّان
dahhaan

خَبّازة
khabbaaza

العائلة
al-'aaila

إِبن
ibn
أخ
akh

اِبنة
ibna
أُخت
ukht

أُم
umm
زوجة
zawja

أب
ab
زوج
zawj

عَمّ \ خال عَمّة \ خالة
amma / khaala amm / khaal

حَيَوان منزلي
hayawaan manzilee

اِبن عم \ اِبن خال
ibn amm / ibn khaal

جَدّ
jadd

جَدّة
jadda

عمل أشياء 'amaal 'ashyaa'

ضَحك
dahik

إبتِسام
ibtisaam

بُكاء
bukaa'

تَفكير
tafkeer

سَماع
samaa'

إمساك
imsaak

رَمي
ramee

گَسر
kasr

رَسم
rasm

كِتابة
kitaaba

قَطع
qat'

قَص
qass

أَكل
akl

تَكلُّم
takallum

حَفر
hafr

حَمل
haml

شُرب
shurb

صُنع
sun'a

قَفز
qafz

رَقص
raqs

غَسل
ghasl

حِياكة
hiyaaka

زَحف
zahf

لَعب
la'ib

مُشاهَدة
mushaahada

تَسَلُّق
tasalluq

شِجار
shijaar

نوم
nawm

أخذ
akhth

قَفَز بالحَبل
qafz bil-habl

خِياطة
khiyaata

إنتظار
intithaar

طَبخ
tabkh

إختباء
ikhtibaa'

قِراءة
qiraa'a

شراء
shiraa'

دَفع
daf'

غِناء
ghinaa'

نَفخ
nafkh

شَدّ
shadd

كَنس
kans

قَطف
qatf

سقوط
suqoot

مَشي
mashee

رَكَض
rakd

جُلوس
juloos

43

الأضداد al-ad-daad

بَعيد
ba'eed

قَريب
qareeb

جَيِّد
jayyid

سيء
say-yi

بارِد
baarid

ساخِن
saakhin

مُبلّل
muballal

جاف
jaaf

أعلى
a'laa

أسفل
asfal

فَوق
fawk

تَحت
taht

سمين
sameen

نَحيف
naheef

وَسِخ
wasikh

نظيف
natheef

صَغير
sagheer

كَبير
kabeer

قَليل
qaleel

كَثير
katheer

مَفتوح
maftouh

مُغلَق
mughlaq

أوَّل
awwal

أخير
akheer

يَسار
yasaar

خارِج
khaarij

داخِل
daakhil

سَهل
sahl

صَعب
sa'ab

فارِغ
faarigh

مَليء
malee'

مريح
mareeh

قاسٍ
qaasin

أمام
amaam

مُرتفِع
murtafi'

بَطيء
batee'

سَريع
saree'

وراء
waraa'

طَويل
taweel

مُنخفِض
munkhafid

قَصير
qaseer

مَيِّت
mayyit

حي
hay

مُظلِم
muthlim

مُضيء
mudee'

قَديم
qadeem

أعلى الدرج
a'laa-d-daraj

يَمين
yameen

جَديد
jadeed

أسفل الدرج
asfal-ud-daraj

45

الأيّام al-ayyaam

الأحد
al-ahad

الخَميس
al-khamees

الثُلاثاء
al-thulaathaa'

الأربِعاء
al-arbi'aa'

الإثنين
al-ithnayn

الجُمعة
al-jum'a

السَبت
as-sabt

تَقويم
taqweem

نَهار
nahaar

مَساء
masaa'

شَمس
shams

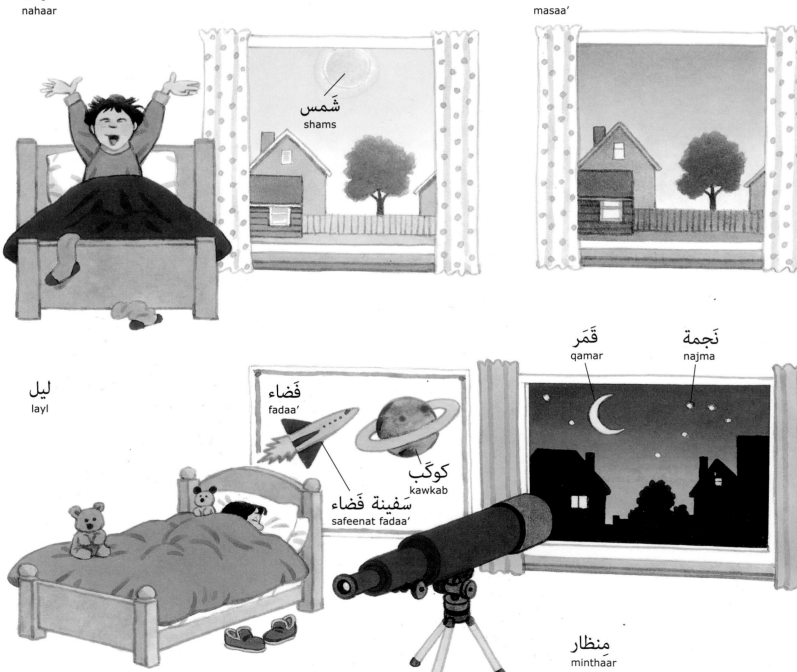

ليل
layl

فَضاء
fadaa'

كوكَب
kawkab

سَفينة فَضاء
safeenat fadaa'

قَمَر
qamar

نَجمة
najma

مِنظار
minthaar

46

الأعياد

al-a'yaad

عيد ميلاد
'eed meelaad

هَدية
hadiyya

شَمعة
sham'a

بِطاقات عيد ميلاد
bitaaqaat 'eed meelaad

كَعكة عيد ميلاد
ka'kat eed meelaad

عُطلة
'otla

يوم الزَفاف
yawm uz-zafaaf

ضُيوف
duyoof

آلة تصوير
aalat tasweer

وَصيفة
waseefa

عَروس
'aroos

عَريس
'arees

مُصَوِّر
musawwir

عيد الميلاد
'eed ul-meelaad

الرنّة
ar-ranna

بابا نويل
baabaa noweel

زلاجة
zallaaja

شَجَرة عيد الميلاد
shajarat 'eed ul-meelaad

الطَّقس at-taqs

شَمس
shams

غيوم
ghuyoom

سَماء
samaa'

مَظَلة
mithala

مَطَر
matar

بَرْق
barq

ضباب
dabaab

ثَلج
thalj

نَدى
nadaa

ريح
reeh

سديم
sadeem

صقيع
saqee'

قوس قُزَح
qaws quzah

الفُصول al-fusool

رَبيع
rabee'

صيف
sayf

خَريف
khareef

شِتاء
shitaa'

48

حَيَوانات مَنزِلية
hayawaanaat manziliya

همستر
hamster

بيطَرية
baytariya

بيت الكَلب
bayt ul-kalb

خَنزير هِندي
khanzeer hindi

ببّغاء صَغيرة
babbaghaa' sagheera

كَلب
kalb

جَرو
jaroo

أكل
akl

ببّغاء
babbaghaa'

مِنقار
minqaar

أرنَب
arnab

كَنار
kanar

قَفَص
qafas

هِرة
hirra

سَلّة
salla

هُرَيرة
huraira

فأر
fa'r

حَليب
haleeb

سَمَك ذَهَبي
samak thahabee

49

الرياضة

ar-riyaada

الشِراع
ash-shiraa'

تَجديف
tajdeef

كُرة السَلّة
kurat us-salla

لَوح تَزلُّج
lawh tazalluj

إبحار شِراعي
ibhaar shiraa'ee

لوح شِراعي
lawh shiraa'ee

كريكِت
kreekit

مَضْرَب
madrab

گَراتي
karaatee

مضْرَب
madrab

كُرة المضرب
kurat ul-madrib

كُرة قَدَم أمريكية
kurat qadam amreekiya

جُمباز
jumbaaz

كُرة
kura

صنارة
sunnara

طُعم
tu'm

رَقْص
raqs

كُرة القاعِدة
kurat ul-qaa'ida

صيد سَمَك
sayd samak

رُغْبي
rugby

غوص
ghaws

مَسْبَح
masbah

سِباق الرَكْض
sibaaq ur-rak...

سِباحة
sibaaha

رَمي بالقوس
ramee bil-qaws

مَرْمى
marma

طيران شِراعي
tayaraan shiraa'ee

خوذة
khootha

رَكض
rakd

دَراجات هَوائية
darraajat hawaa'iya

تَسَلُّق
tasalluq

جودو
joodo

حِصان
hisaan

فَرَس
faras

خَزنة
khazna

كُرة القَدَم
kurat ul-qadm

كُرة الريشة
kurat ur-reesha

فُروسية
furoosiya

غرفة تغيير الملابس
ghurfat taghyeer ul-malaabis

كُرة الطاولة
kurat ut-taawila

مَزالج
mazaalij

تَزَلُّج جَليدي
tazalluj jaleedee

عصا تَزَلُّج
'asaa tazalluj

مقْعَد هَوائي
maq'ad hawaa'ee

مَزالج
mazaalij

تَزَلُّج على الثَلج
tazalluj 'alaa th-thalj

مُصارعة سومو
musaara'at soomoo

51

الألوان al-alwaan

بُرتُقالي
burtuqaalee

أخضَر
akhdar

أسوَد
aswad

رَمادي
ramaadee

أحمَر
ahmar

بُنّي
bunnee

وَردي
wardee

بَنَفْسَجي
banafsajee

أصفَر
asfar

أبيَض
abyad

أزرَق
azraq

الأشكال al-ashkaal

مُستَطيل
mustateel

دائرة
daa'ira

مَعين
ma'een

مَخروط
makhroot

نَجمة
najma

مُكَعَّب
muka''ab

بَيضوي
baydawee

مُثَلَّث
muthallath

مُرَبَّع
murabba'

هلال
hilaal

52

الأعداد al-a'daad

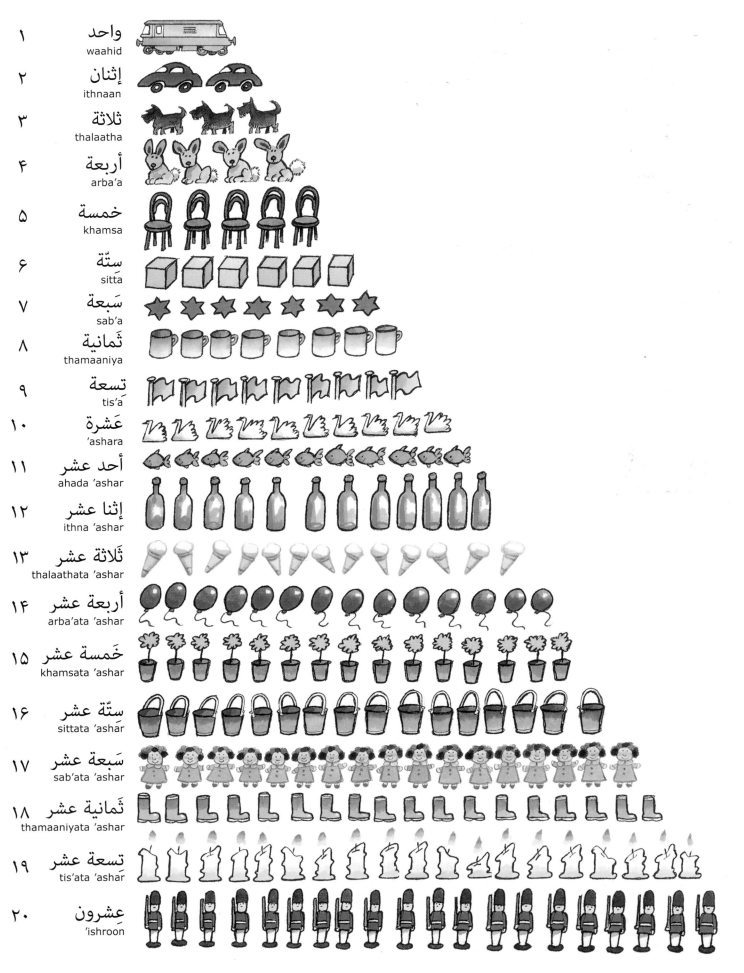

١	واحد waahid
٢	إثنان ithnaan
٣	ثلاثة thalaatha
٤	أربعة arba'a
٥	خمسة khamsa
٦	سِتّة sitta
٧	سَبعة sab'a
٨	ثَمانية thamaaniya
٩	تسعة tis'a
١٠	عَشرة 'ashara
١١	أحد عشر ahada 'ashar
١٢	إثنا عشر ithna 'ashar
١٣	ثَلاثة عشر thalaathata 'ashar
١٤	أربعة عشر arba'ata 'ashar
١٥	خَمسة عشر khamsata 'ashar
١٦	ستّة عشر sittata 'ashar
١٧	سَبعة عشر sab'ata 'ashar
١٨	ثَمانية عشر thamaaniyata 'ashar
١٩	تسعة عشر tis'ata 'ashar
٢٠	عِشرون 'ishroon

مَدينة المَلاهي
madeenat al-malaahee

دولاب كَبير
doolaab kabeer

دَوارة
dawaara

غَزل نَبات
ghazl nabaat

زُحلوقة عملاقة
zuhlooqa 'imlaaqa

قطار الرُعب
qitaar ur-ru'b

فُشار
fushaar

حَصيرة
haseera

سيارات مُتَصادِمة
sayaarat mutasaadima

حَلَقات
halaqaat

أفعوانية
uf'uwaaniyya

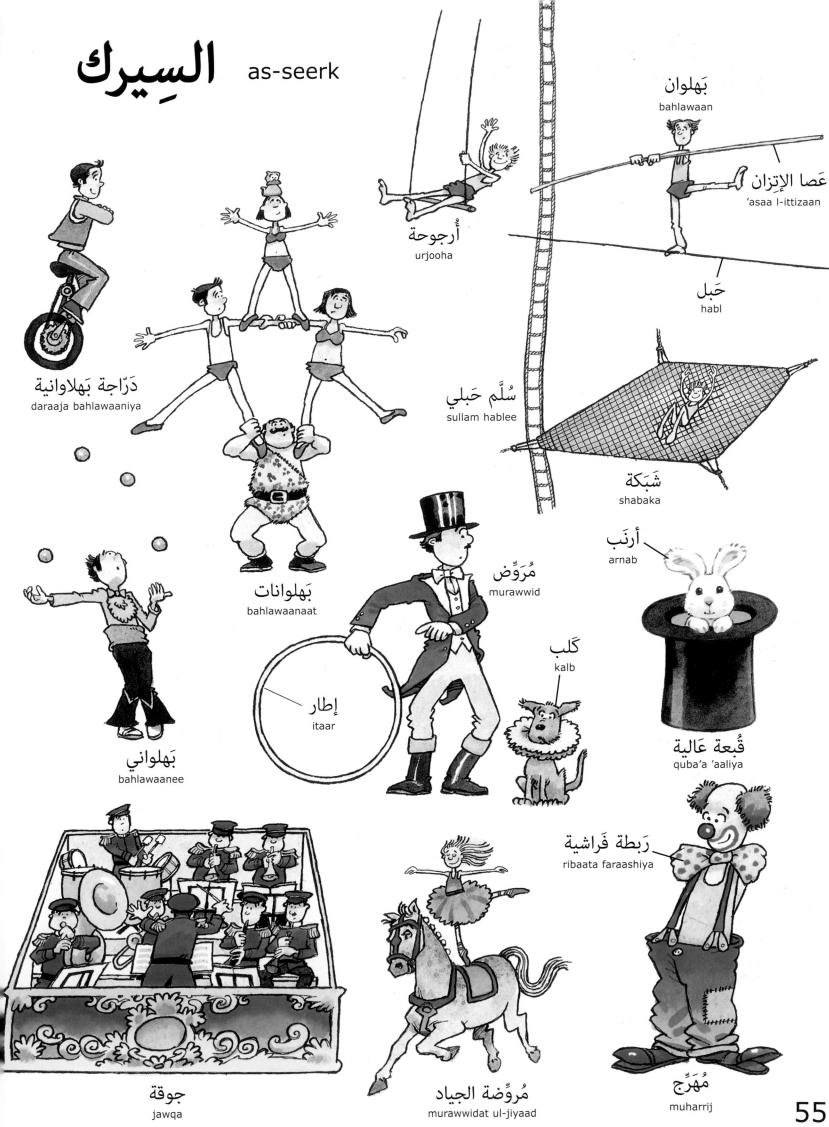

السِيرك as-seerk

بَهلوان
bahlawaan

عَصا الإتِزان
'asaa l-ittizaan

أُرجوحة
urjooha

حَبل
habl

دَرّاجة بَهلاوانية
daraaja bahlawaaniya

سُلَّم حَبلي
sullam hablee

شَبَكة
shabaka

أرنَب
arnab

بَهلوانات
bahlawaanaat

مُرَوِّض
murawwid

قُبعة عَالية
quba'a 'aaliya

كَلب
kalb

بَهلواني
bahlawaanee

إطار
itaar

رَبطة فَراشية
ribaata faraashiya

جوقة
jawqa

مُرَوِّضة الجياد
murawwidat ul-jiyaad

مُهَرِّج
muharrij

Word list

On these pages you will find all the Arabic words in the book, in order of the Arabic alphabet. Next to each word, you can see its pronunciation in Roman letters (the letters we use to write English), and then its meaning in English. Remember that Arabic is read from right to left.

The Arabic alphabet

There are twenty-eight letters in the Arabic alphabet. These are almost all consonants, as the vowel sounds (such as **a** or **u**) are shown by signs called *harakat* above or below the letters. Arabic letters are written slightly differently when they are joined together in words, depending on whether they are at the beginning or in the middle or at the end of a word.

Name of letter	Arabic letter	Pronunciation
alif	ا	**aa** as in **father**
ba	ب	**b** as in **bag**
ta	ت	**t** as in **tag**
tha	ث	**th** as in **thin**
jeem	ج	**j** as in **jeans**
ha	ح	an **h** sound made in your throat. Listen to an Arabic speaker to hear how to say it.
kha	خ	like the **ch** in the Scottish word **loch**
dal	د	**d** as in **dog**
dhal	ذ	**th** as in **then**
ra	ر	**r** as in **rock**
zein	ز	**z** as in **zoo**
seen	س	**s** as in **sun**
sheen	ش	**sh** as in **sheep**
sad	ص	a strong **s** sound
dad	ض	a strong **d** sound
ta	ط	a strong **t** sound
za	ظ	a strong **th** sound as in **that**
ayn	ع	There is no sound exactly like this in English; it is shown as **a'** or **i'** in this book depending on the *harakat*. Listen to an Arabic speaker to hear how to say it.
ghayn	غ	like the French **r** sound
fa	ف	**f** as in **far**
qaf	ق	a strong **k** sound, made at the back of your throat
kaf	ك	**k** as in **king**
lam	ل	**l** as in **look**
meem	م	**m** as in **man**
noon	ن	**n** as in **now**
ha	ه	**h** as in **him**
waw	و	**w** as in **wish**
yaw	ي	**y** as in **yes**

There is also the *hamza* (' in the pronunciation), which can appear on its own or with an *alif* to make the following sounds:

ء on its own, the *hamza* means there is a break in the word

أ with a *fatha* (see below), it is pronounced **u** as in **up**

أُ with a *damma*, it is pronounced **oo** as in **wool**

إ with a *kasra*, it is pronounced **i** as in **if**.

Vowels and other letter sounds

Three *harakat* are used to show vowel sounds:

  ﹷ *fatha* (a short line above the letter): this gives an **a** sound, as is **man**

  ﹹ *damma* (a small *waw*, و above the letter): this gives an **oo** sound, as in **soot**

  kasra (a short line below the letter): this gives an **i** sound, as in **sit**.

There are two more *harakat*:

  ﹿ *sukoon* (a small circle above the letter) shows that there is no vowel sound

  ﹽ *shadda* (a small "w" shape above the letter) shows that the letter is stressed.

ا				أقنعة	aqni'a	masks
أب	ab	father		أكْتاف	aktaaf	shoulders
إبتِسام	ibtisaam	smiling		الأكل	al-akl	food
إبحار شِراعي	ibhaar shiraa'ee	sailing		أكل	akl	food, eating
إبريق شاي	ibreeq shaay	teapot, kettle		أكواب	akwaab	glasses
إبزيم	ibzeem	buckle		أكياس	akyaas	carrier bags
إبن	ibn	son		آلة التذاكِر	aalat ut-tathaakir	ticket machine
إبن خال	ibn khaal	cousin – mother's side		آلة تصوير	aalat tasweer	camera
				ألعاب	al'aab	toys
إبن عَمّ	ibn amm	cousin – father's side		ألعاب نارية	al'aab naariya	fireworks
إبنة	ibna	daughter		ألوان	alwaan	paints
إبهام	ibhaam	thumb		الألوان	al-alwaan	colours
أبْيَض	abyad	white		ألوان شَمع	alwaan sham'	crayons
إثنا عشر	ithna 'ashar	twelve		أم	umm	mother
إثنان	ithnan	two		أمام	amaam	front
الإثنين	al-ithnayn	Monday		إمرأة	imra'a	woman
إجّاص	ijjas	pear		إمساك	imsaak	catching
الأحد	al-ahad	Sunday		أمواج	amwaaj	waves
أحد عشر	ahada 'ashar	eleven		أنا	ana	me
أحذية تَزلُّج	ahthiyat tazalluj	roller blades		أنابيب	anaabeeb	pipes
أحمَر	ahmar	red		أناناس	anaanaas	pineapple
أخ	akh	brother		إنتظار	intithaar	waiting
أخت	ukht	sister		إنسان آلي	insaan aaliee	robot
إختباء	ikhtibaa'	hiding		أنف	anf	nose
أخذ	akhth	taking		أوراق شَجَر	awraaq shajar	leaves
أخضَر	akhdar	green		إوِزّ	iwazz	geese
أخير	akheer	last		أوّل	awwal	first
أدراج	adraaj	steps		الأيّام	al-ayyaam	days
آذان	aathaan	ears		أيل	ayl	deer
الأربِعاء	al-arbi'aa'	Wednesday				
أربعة	arba'a	four		**ب**		
أربعة عشر	arba'ata 'ashar	fourteen		باب	baab	door
أرجوحة	urjooha	trapeze		بابا نويل	baabaa noweel	Father Christmas
أرجوحة	orjooha	swings		بارد	baarid	cold
أُرُز	aruz	rice		بازَلاء	bazillaa'	peas
أرضية	ardiya	floor		بالون	baaloon	balloon
أرنب	arnab	rabbit		بَبّغاء	babbaghaa'	parrot
أريكة	areeka	sofa		بَبّغاء صَغيرة	babbaghaa' sagheera	budgerigar
أزرَق	azraq	blue		بيتزة	bitza	pizza
أزهار	azhaar	flowers		بَجَعة	baja'a	pelican, swans
أزياء تَنَكُّرية	azyaa' tanakkuriya	fancy dress		بَحّار	bahhaar	sailor
أستاذة	ustaatha	teacher		بَحر	bahr	sea
أسَد	asad	lion		بُحيرة	buhaira	lake
إسطَبل	istabl	stable		بُذور	budhoor	seeds
أسفل	asfal	bottom		بُراغي صغيرة	baraaghee sagheera	screws
أسفل الدرج	'asfal-ud-daraj	downstairs		بُرتَقالة	burtuqaala	orange (fruit)
أسنان	asnaan	teeth		بُرتُقالي	burtuqaalee	orange (colour)
أسوَد	aswad	black		بُرج المُراقَبة	burj ul-muraaqaba	control tower
إشارات ضوئية	ishaaraat daw'iya	traffic lights, signals		بُرغُر	burger	hamburger
أشبال	ashbaal	cubs		بَرق	barq	lightning
الأشكال	al-ashkaal	shapes		بِركة	birka	pond
أصابِع	asaabi'	fingers		بَرميل	barmeel	barrel
أصابِع القَدَم	asaabi' al-qadam	toes		بُرَيْكة	burayka	puddle
أصفَر	asfar	yellow		بِساط	bisaat	rug
الأضداد	al-ad-daad	opposites		البُستان	al-bustaan	garden
أضواء أمامية	adwaa' amaamiya	headlights		بُستان فاكِهة	bustaan faakiha	orchard
إطار	itaar	hoop		بَسكوت	baskoot	biscuit
أطفال	atfaal	children		بَصَل	basal	onion
الأعداد	al-a'dad	numbers		بَطّارية	battariya	battery
أعشاب	a'shaab	grass		بَطاطا	bataata	potatoes
أعلى	a'laa	top		بَطاطا مَقلية	bataata maqliya	chips
أعلى الدرج	a'laa-d-daraj	upstairs		بَطاطا مَهروسة	bataata mahroosa	mashed potatoes
الأعياد	al-a'yaad	special days		بِطاقات	bitaaqaat	cards
أفعوانية	uf'uwaaniyya	rollercoaster		بِطاقات عيد ميلاد	bitaaqaat 'eed meelaad	birthday card
أقراص خُبز	aqraas khubz	rolls				
أقراص دَواء	aqraas dawaa'	pills		بَطة	batta	ducks
أقلام لبّاد	aqlaam labbad	felt-tips		بَطريق	batreeq	penguin

57

بَطن	batn	tummy
بَطيء	batee'	slow
بَعيد	ba'eed	far
البِقالة	al-biqaala	shop
بَقَرة	baqara	cow
بُكاء	bukaa'	crying
بَلاط	balaat	tiles
بِنت	bint	girl
بَندة	panda	panda
بَندورة	banadoora	tomato
بَنزين	banzeen	petrol
بَنَفسَجي	banafsajee	purple
بُنّي	bunnee	brown
بَهلَوان	bahlawaan	tightrope walker
بَهلَوانات	bahlawaanat	acrobats
بَهلَواني	bahlawaanee	juggler
بوابة	bawwaaba	gate
بوظة	bootha	ice cream
بوق	booq	trumpet
بومة	booma	owl
بيانو	piyanoo	piano
بيت الكَلب	bayt ul-kalb	kennel
بيت بلاستيك	bayt plaasteek	greenhouse
بيت مُتنقّل	bayt mutanakkel	caravan
بيض	bayd	eggs
بيض مَسلوق	bayd maslooq	boiled egg
بيض مقلي	bayd maqlee	fried egg
بَيضوي	baydawee	oval
بيطَرية	baytariya	vet

ت

تِبن	tibn	hay
تَجديف	tajdeef	rowing
تَحت	taht	under
تُراب	turaab	earth
تَزَلّج جَليدي	tazalluj jaleedee	ice skating
تَزَلّج على الثَلج	tazalluj 'alaa th-thalj	skiing
تَزَلّج مائي	tazalluj maa'ee	water-skier
تسعة	tis'a	nine
تسعة عشر	tis'ata 'ashar	nineteen
تَسَلّق	tasalluq	climbing
تُفّاحة	tuffaaha	apple
تَفكير	tafkeer	thinking
تَقويم	taqweem	calendar
تَكَلّم	takallum	talking
تَلّ	tal	hill
تلفزيون	televiziyoon	television
تمثال	timthaal	statue
تِمساح	timsaah	crocodile
تَنّورة	tannoora	skirt
توت	toot	raspberry

ث

ثَعلب	tha'lab	fox
الثُلاثاء	ath-thulaathaa'	Tuesday
ثلاثة	thalaatha	three
ثلاثة عشر	thalaathata 'ashar	thirteen
ثَلاجة	thallaaja	fridge
ثَلج	thalj	snow
ثمانية	thamaaniya	eight
ثمانية عشر	thamaaniyata 'ashar	eighteen
ثور	thawr	bull
ثور أمريكي	thawr amreekee	bison

ج

| جاف | jaaf | dry |
| جِبس | jibs | plaster |

جَبَل	jabal	mountain
جبنة	jubna	cheese
جَدّ	jadd	grandfather
جَدّة	jadda	grandmother
جَدوَل	jadwal	stream
جَديد	jadeed	new
جذوع الشَجر	juthoo' ush-shajar	logs
جِراء ثَعلب	jiraa' tha'lab	fox cubs
جَرّار	jarrar	tractor
جَرّافة	jarraafa	digger
جُرف	jurf	cliff
جَرو	jaroo	puppy
جَريدة	jareeda	newspaper
جَزَر	jazar	carrot
جَزمة	jazma	boots
جَزيرة	jazeera	island
جِسر	jisr	bridge
جُلوس	juloos	sitting
جُمباز	jumbaaz	gym
الجُمعة	al-jum'a	Friday
جَمَل	jamal	camel
جَناح	janaah	wing
جنود دُمى	junood dumaa	soldiers
جِهاز تَدفِئة	jihaz tadfi'ah	radiator
جوارِب	jawaarib	socks
جودو	joodo	judo
جَورب طويل	jawrab taweel	tights
جوقة	jawqa	band
جيتار	geetar	guitar
جَيِّد	jayyid	good
جينز	jeens	jeans
جيوب	juyoob	pockets

ح

حائط	haa'it	wall
حاجِب	haajib	eyebrow
حاسوب	hasoob	computer
حافِلة	haafila	bus
حَبَل	habl	rope, tightrope
حَبَل القَفز	habl ul-qafz	skipping rope
حِجارة	hijaara	stones
الحَديقة العامة	al-hadeeqat ul-'aamma	park
حِذاء	hithaa'	shoes
حِذاء رياضي	hithaa' riyaadi	trainers
الحُروف الأَبجَدية	al-huroof ul-abjadiya	alphabet
حِزام	hizaam	belt
حُزَم التِبن	huzam ut-tibn	straw bales
حَساء	hasaa'	soup
حِساب	hisaab	sums
حَصّالة	hassaala	money box
حِصان	hisaan	horse
حِصان هزاز	hisaan hazzaz	rocking horse
حَصى	hasaa	pebbles
حَصيرة	haseera	mat
حَظيرة	hatheera	barn
حَظيرة الخَنازير	hatheerat ul-khanaazeer	pigsty
حَظيرة بَقر	hatheerat baqar	cowshed
حَفّارة	haffaara	road drill
حِفاض	hifaad	nappy
حَفر	hafr	digging
حُفرة	hufra	hole
الحَفلة	al-hafla	party
حَقل	haql	field
حَقيبة	haqeeba	suitcase
حَقيبة الظَهر	haqeebat uth-thaher	backpack

حَقيبة يد	haqeebat yad	handbag
حَلّاق	hallaaq	hairdresser
حَلَزون	halazoon	snail
حَلَقات	halaqaat	hoop-la
حَلوى	halwaa	sweet
حلويّات	halwiyyaat	pudding
حَليب	haleeb	milk
حِمار	himaar	donkey
حِمار وَحشي	himaar wahshee	zebra
حَمّام	hammaam	bathroom
حَمامة	hamaama	pigeon
حَمل	haml	carrying
حوت	hoot	whale
حَوض الجلي	hawd ul-jali	sink
حوض رَمل	hawd raml	sandpit
حَوض زَرع	hawdu zar'	flower bed
حوض سَمَك	hawd samak	aquarium
حى	hay	alive
حِياكة	hiyaaka	knitting
حية	hayya	snake
حَيَوان منزلي	hayawaan manzilee	pet
الحيوانات	al-hayawaanaat	animals
حيوانات مَنزلية	hayawaanaat manziliya	pets

خ

خاتم	khaatim	ring
خارِج	khaarij	out
خال	khaal	uncle – mother's side
خالة	khaala	aunt – mother's side
خَبّازة	khabbaaza	baker
خُبز	khubz	bread
خُبز مُحَمَّص	khubz muhammas	toast
خَد	khadd	cheek
خَرَز	kharaz	beads
خَرطوم	khartoom	trunk
خُرطوم	khurtoom	hosepipe
خِرفان	khirfaan	sheep
خَريطة	khareeta	map
خَريف	khareef	autumn
خَزانة	khazaana	wardrobe
خَزانة حائط	khazaanat haa'it	cupboard
خَزنة	khazna	locker
خَس	khass	lettuce
خضار و فواكه	khudar wa fawaikeh	vegetables and fruit
خُضروات	khudrawaat	vegetables
خَفّاش	khaffaash	bat
خُلد	khuld	mole
خَليّة نحل	khaliyat nahl	beehive
خمسة	khamsa	five
خمسة عشر	khamsata 'ashar	fifteen
الخَميس	al-khamees	Thursday
خَنازير	khanaazeer	pigs
خَنانيص	khanaanees	piglets
خَوخ	khawkh	plum
خوذة	khootha	helmet
خِيار	khiyaar	cucumber
خِياطة	khiyaata	sewing
خِيام	khiyaam	tents
خِيطان	khitaan	string

د

دائرة	daa'ira	circle
داخِل	daakhil	in
دار	daar	house
دار السينِما	dar us-seenima	cinema

دار دُمى	dar dumaa	doll's house
دُبّ	dubb	bear, teddy bear
دُبّ قُطبي	dubb qutbee	polar bear
دَبّور	dabboor	wasp
دَجاج	dajaaj	hens, (cooked) chicken
دُخان	dukhaan	smoke
دَرّاجات هَوائية	darraajat hawaa'iya	cycling
دَرّاجة	darraaja	bicycle
دَرّاجة بَهلاوانية	darraaja bahlawaaniya	trick cyclist
دَرّاجة ثُلاثية	darraaja thulaathiya	tricycle
دَرّاجة نارية	darraaja naariya	motorbike
دُرّاق	durraq	peach
دُرج	durj	drawer
دَرَج	daraj	stairs
دُعسوقة	du'sooqa	ladybird
دَفتَر	daftar	notebook
دَفع	daf'	pushing
دُكّان	dukkaan	shop
دُكّان الألعاب	dukkaan ul-al'aab	toyshop
دُلفين	dolfeen	dolphin
دُمى	dumaa	dolls
دَهّان	dahhaan	painter
دهان الوجه	dihaan-ul- wajh	face paints
دَواء	dawaa'	medicine
دَوّارة	dawaara	roundabout
دودة	dooda	caterpillar
دودة أرض	doodat ard	worm
دولاب	doolaab	tyre
دولاب كَبير	doolab kabeer	big wheel
دولاب هواء	doolaab hawa'	windmill
ديك	deek	cockerel
ديوك حَبش	duyook habash	turkeys

ذ

ذِئب	th'ib	wolf
ذُبابة	thubaaba	fly
ذراع	thiraa'	arm
ذَقَن	thaqn	chin
ذَيل	thayl	tail

ر

رائد فَضاء	raaid fadaa'	astronaut
رأس	ra's	head
رافِعة	raafi'a	crane
راقِص	raaqis	dancer – man
راقِصة	raaqisa	dancer – woman
رِباط	ribaat	shoelace
رباطة فَراشية	ribaata faraashiya	bow tie
رَبطة عنق	rabtat 'unuq	tie
رَبيع	rabee'	spring
رَجُل	rajul	man
رجل	rijl	leg
رَجُل إطفاء	rajul itfaa'	fireman
رِداء	ridaa'	dressing gown
رَسائل	rasaa'il	letters
رَسم	rasm	drawing, painting
رَسَن	rasan	lead
رَشاش ماء	rashaash maa'	sprinkler
رَصيف	raseef	pavement, platform
رَضيع	radee'	baby
رُغبي	rugby	rugby
رقائق الحبوب	raqa'iq-ul-huboob	cereal
رَقَبة	raqaba	neck
رَقص	raqs	dance, dancing
رُكبة	rukba	knee

رَكض	*rakd*	running
رَكض	*rakd*	running, jogging
رَمادي	*ramadee*	grey
رَمي	*ramee*	throwing
رَمي بالقوس	*ramee bil qaws*	archery
الرنّة	*ar-ranna*	reindeer
روّاد فضاء	*ruwwaad fadaa'*	spacemen
الرياضة	*ar-riyaadha*	sport and exercise
ريح	*reeh*	wind
ريش	*reesh*	feathers
ريشة	*reesha*	brush
الريف	*ar-reef*	country

ز

زبالة	*zibaala*	rubbish, dustbin
زُبدة	*zubda*	butter
زُجاجات	*zujaajaat*	bottles
زَحف	*zahf*	crawling
زُحلوقة	*zuhlooqa*	slide
زُحلوقة عملاقة	*zuhlooqa 'imlaaqa*	helter-skelter
زرّ	*zirr*	buttons
زَرافة	*zaraafa*	giraffe
زعانف	*za'aanif*	flippers
زلّاجَة	*zallaaja*	sleigh
زَهر	*zahr*	dice
زوج	*zawj*	husband
زوجة	*zawja*	wife
زورَق	*zawraq*	rowing boat, canoe
زيت	*zayt*	oil

س

سائق القطار	*saa'iq ul-qitaar*	train driver
سائق حَافلة	*saa'iq haafila*	bus driver
سائقة شاحِنة	*saaiqat shaahina*	lorry driver
ساخِن	*saakhin*	hot
ساعة حائط	*saa'at ha'it*	clock
ساعة يد	*saa'at yad*	watch
ساعي البريد	*saa'i-l bareed*	postman
سباحة	*sibaaha*	swimming
سِباق الرَكض	*sibaaq ur-rakd*	race
سَبانخ	*sabaanikh*	spinach
السَبت	*as-sabt*	Saturday
سبعة	*sab'a*	seven
سبعة عشر	*sab'ata 'ashar*	seventeen
ستار	*sitaar*	blind, curtain
سِتة	*sitta*	six
ستة عشر	*sittata 'ashar*	sixteen
سُترة	*sutra*	jacket
سُترة صوف	*sutrat soof*	cardigan
سَجّادة	*sajjada*	carpet
سُجُق	*sujuq*	salami
سَحّاب	*sahhaab*	zip
سحليّة	*sihliyya*	lizard
سَدّ	*sadd*	lock
سديم	*sadeem*	mist
سَرج	*sarj*	saddle
سَرَطان	*sarataan*	crab
سروال	*sirwaal*	trousers
سروال داخلي	*sirwaal daakhilee*	pants
سروال قَصير	*sirwaal qaseer*	shorts
سرير	*sareer*	bed
سَريع	*saree'*	fast
سَطل	*satl*	bucket
السَفَر	*as-safar*	travel
سفينة	*safeena*	ship
سفينة فَضاء	*safeenat fadaa'*	spaceship
سَقف	*saqf*	roof, ceiling

سقوط	*suqoot*	falling
سَكاكين	*sakaakeen*	knives
سِكّة حَديد	*sikkat hadeed*	railway track
سُكّر	*sukkar*	sugar
سَلّة	*salla*	basket
سَلة المُهمَلات	*sallat ul-muhmalaat*	wastepaper bin
سُلحفاة	*sulhafaa*	tortoise
سَلَطة	*salata*	salad
سُلّم	*sullam*	ladder
سُلّم حَبلي	*sullam hablee*	rope ladder
سَماء	*samaa'*	sky
سَماع	*samaa'*	listening
سَمَك	*samak*	fish
سَمَك ذَهَبي	*samak thahabee*	goldfish
سَمَك قرش	*samak qirsh*	shark
سَمّور	*sammoor*	beaver
سَمين	*sameen*	fat
سنجاب	*sinjaab*	squirrel
سِهام	*sihaam*	arrows
سَهل	*sahl*	easy
سوق	*sooq*	market
سيء	*say-yi'*	bad
سِياج	*siyaaj*	railings, fence, hedge
سيارات مُتَصادمة	*sayyaarat mutasaadima*	dodgems
سيارة	*sayyaara*	car
سيارة أُجرة	*sayyaarat ujra*	taxi
سيارة إسعاف	*sayyaarat is'aaf*	ambulance
سيارة الإطفاء	*sayyaarat ul-itfaa'*	fire engine
سيارة الشُرطة	*sayyaarat ush-shurta*	police car
سيارة تصليح	*sayyaarat tasleeh*	breakdown lorry
سيارة سباق	*sayyaarat sibaaq*	racing car
سيارة شحن	*sayyaarat shahn*	van
السيرك	*as-seerk*	circus

ش

شاحِنة	*shaahina*	lorry
شاحِنة صهريج	*shaahinat sahreej*	tanker
شاحِنة نفط	*shaahinat nift*	petrol tanker
شارَة	*shaara*	badge
الشارع	*ash-shaari'*	street
شاطىء	*shaati'*	beach
شاطىء البَحر	*shaati' ul-bahr*	seaside
شال	*shaal*	scarf
شاي	*shaay*	tea
شَبَكة	*shabaka*	net, safety net
شتاء	*shitaa'*	winter
شِجار	*shijaar*	fighting
شَجَر	*shajar*	trees
شَجَرة	*shajara*	tree
شَجَرة عيد الميلاد	*shajarat 'eed ul-meelaad*	Christmas tree
شجيرة	*shujayra*	bush
شَدّ	*shadd*	pulling
شراء	*shiraa'*	buying
شرائح البطاطا	*sharaa'ih ul-bataata*	crisps
شُرب	*shurb*	drinking
شَرشَف	*sharshaf*	sheet
الشرطي	*ash-shurtee*	policeman
الشُرطيَة	*ash-shurtiya*	policewoman
شَريطة	*shareeta*	bow
شَطيرة	*shateera*	sandwich
شَعر	*sh'ar*	hair
شفاه	*shifaah*	lips
شُقَق	*shooqaq*	flats
شَلال	*shallaal*	waterfall

شمّام	shammaam	melon
شمس	shams	sun
شمسية	shamsiya	umbrella
شمعة	sham'a	candle
شُوَك	shuwak	forks
شوكة	shawka	fork
شوكولاتة	shokolaata	chocolate
شوكولاتة ساخِنة	shokolaata saakhina	hot chocolate

ص

صابون	saaboon	soap
صاروخ	saarookh	rocket
صُحون	suhoon	plates
صُحون صغيرة	suhoon sagheera	saucers
صَخرة جليد	sakhrat jaleed	iceberg
صُخور	sukhoor	rocks
صَدر	sadr	chest
صَدَفة	sadafa	shell
صعب	sa'ab	difficult
صغير	sagheer	small
صَفّارة	saffara	whistle
صَقر	saqr	eagle
صقيع	saqee'	frost
صلصة بَندورة	salsat banadoora	ketchup
صنارة	sunnara	fishing rod
صُنبور	sunboor	tap
صندل	sandal	sandals
صُندوق	sundooq	box, boot
صُندوق الأدوات	sundooq ul-adwaat	toolbox
صُندوق الدَفع	sundooq ad-daf'	checkout
صُنع	sun'a	making
صَوامِل	sawaamil	nuts
صُوان	sowan	chest of drawers
صُوَر	suwar	photographs
صَيّاد سَمَك	sayyaad samak	fisherman
صيد سَمَك	sayd samak	fishing
صيصان	seesaan	chicks
صيف	sayf	summer
صينية	seeniya	tray

ض

ضَباب	dabaab	fog
ضَحك	dahik	laughing
ضفدَع	difda'	frog
ضَماد	dimaad	bandage
ضَماد لاصِق	dimaad laasiq	sticking plaster
ضُيوف	duyoof	guests

ط

طائرة	taa'ira	plane
طائرة مروحيّة	taa'ira mirwahiyya	helicopter
طاسات	taasaat	bowls
طاقَم الطائرة	taakam ut-taa'ira	cabin crew
طاقية	taaqiya	cap
طاولة	taawila	table
طاوَلة الكي	taawilat ul-kay	ironing board
طاولة نجارة	taawilat nijara	workbench
طَبّاخ	tabbaakh	chef
طَباشير	tabaasheer	chalk
طَبخ	tabkh	cooking
طُبول	tubool	drums
الطبيب	at-tabeeb	the doctor
طبيبة	tabeeba	doctor
طَبيبة أسنان	tabeebat asnaan	dentist
طَحالِب	tahaaleb	seaweed
طَحين	taheen	flour
طَريق	tareeq	road, path

طعم	tu'm	bait
الطَقس	at-taqs	weather
طَناجِر	tanaajir	saucepans
طوب	toob	bricks
طَوق	tawq	necklace
طَويل	taweel	long
طيار	tayyaar	pilot
طيّارة وَرَق	tayyaarat waraq	kite
طيران شراعي	tayaraan shiraa'ee	hang gliding
طين للتَشكيل	teen lit-tashkeel	clay

ظ

ظَهر	thahr	back (of body)

ع

العائلة	al-'aa'ila	families
عُجّة	'ujja	omelette
عجل	'ijl	calf
عَجَلة	'ajala	wheel
عَرائس	'araa'is	puppets
عَرَبة	'araba	trailer, trolley, cart
عَرَبة أطفال	'arabat atfaal	pram, pushchair
عَرَبة يد	'arabat yad	wheelbarrow
عُروة	'urwa	button holes
عَروس	'aroos	bride
عريس	'arees	bridegroom
عَزقات	'azakaat	bolts
عَسَل	'asal	honey
عُش	'ush	nest
عَشاء	ashaa'	supper or dinner
عشرة	'ashara	ten
عشرون	'ishroon	twenty
عصا	'asaa	walking stick
عَصا الإتزان	'asaa l-ittizaan	pole
عصا تَزَلّج	'asaa tazalluj	ski pole
عَصافير	'asaafeer	birds
عصي	'isee	chopsticks
عَصير فَواكه	'aseer fawaakih	fruit juice
عُطلة	'otla	holiday
عَظمة	'athma	bone
عُكّازات	'ukkaazaat	crutches
عَلاقة	'allaaqa	pegs
عُلبة دهان	'ulbat dihaan	paint pot
عُلبة كِبريت	'ulbat kibreet	matches
عَلجوم	'aljoom	toad
عَلَم	'alam	flag
عَمّ	'amm	uncle – father's side
عَمّة	'amma	aunt – father's side
عمل أشياء	'amaal 'ashyaa'	doing things
عَمود الاتجاهات	'amood ul-ittijaahat	signpost
عَمود إنارة	'amood inara	lamp post
عِنَب	'inab	grapes
عَنكبوت	'ankaboot	spider
عيد الميلاد	'eed ul-meelaad	Christmas day
عيد ميلاد	'eed meelaad	birthday
عَين	'ayn	eye

غ

غابة	ghaaba	forest
غَداء	ghadaa'	lunch
غِراء	ghiraa'	glue
غُرفة تغيير الملابس	ghurfat taghyeer ul-malabis	changing room
غُرفة جُلوس	ghurfat julus	living room
غُرفة نوم	ghurfat nawm	bedroom
غريبفروت	graybfroot	grapefruit
غُرَيَّر	ghuraiyr	badger

غَزل نَبات	ghazl nabaat	candy floss
غَسّالة	ghassaala	washing machine
غَسل	ghasl	washing
غُصون	ghusoon	twigs
غِطاء المائدة	ghitaa' ul-maa'ida	tablecloth
غِطاء المُحَرّك	ghitaa' ul-muharrik	bonnet
غُلَل	ghulal	marbles
غِناء	ghinaa'	singing
غَنَم	ghanam	lambs
غَوّاص	ghawwaas	diver
غَوّاصة	ghawwaasa	submarine
غوريلا	ghooreela	gorilla
غوص	ghaws	diving
غيوم	ghuyoom	cloud

ف

فأر	fa'r	mouse
فارة	faara	plane
فارِغ	faarigh	empty
فَأَس	fa's	axe
فاصوليا	fasooliyaa'	beans
فِراخ بط	firakhu batt	ducklings
فِراخ ضَفدع	firakhu difda'	tadpoles
فَراشة	faraasha	butterfly
فَراشة ليل	faraashat layl	moth
فَراولة	faraawla	strawberry
فَرَس	faras	pony
فَرَس البحر	faras ul-bahr	hippopotamus
فُرشاة	furshaa	brush
فُرشاة أسنان	furshaat asnaan	toothbrush
فُرشاة شعر	furshaat sha'r	brush
فُرن	furn	cooker
فُروسية	furoosiya	riding
فَزّاعة	fazzaa'a	scarecrow
فُستان	fustaan	dress
فُشار	fushaar	popcorn
الفُصول	al-fusool	seasons
فَضاء	fadaa'	space
فطائِر	fataa'ir	pancakes
فطر	fitr	mushroom
فُطور	futoor	breakfast
فَقَمة	faqama	seal
فلفِل	filfil	pepper
فَم	fam	mouth
فَناجين	fanaajeen	cups
فنّانة	fannaana	artist
فُندُق	fundooq	hotel
فَهد	fahd	leopard
فواكِه	fawaakih	fruit
فوطة	foota	tea towel
فَوق	fawk	over
فيل	feel	elephant

ق

قارب	qaarib	yacht
قارِب سريع	qaarib saree'	motor boat
قارِب صيد	qaarib sayd	fishing boat
قاسٍ	qaasin	hard
قاضٍ	qaadin	judge
قاطِرة	qaatira	engine
قاعة الانتِظار	qaa'at ul-intithaar	waiting room
قُبّعة	qubba'a	hat
قُبّعة القَش	qubba'at ul-qash	sunhat
قُبّعة عالية	qubba'a 'aaliya	top hat
قَدَم	qadam	foot
قَديم	qadeem	old
قِراءة	qiraa'a	reading

قِرد	qird	monkey
قُرص مُدمَج	qurs modmaj	DVD
قرع	qar'	pumpkin
قَرن	qarn	horns
قَريب	qareeb	near
قَرية	qariya	village
قِشدة	qishda	cream
قَص	qass	cutting
قَصير	qaseer	short
قِطار	qitaar	train
قِطار البَضائع	qitaar ul-badaa'i'	goods train
قِطار الرُعب	qitaar ur-ru'b	ghost train
قِطار كَهربائي	qitaar kahrabaa'ee	train set
قَطع	qat'	chopping
قِطع خَشَب	qita' khashab	wood
قَطف	qatf	picking
قُطن	qutn	cotton wool
قفازان	quffaazaan	gloves
قَفز	qafz	jumping
قَفز بالحَبل	qafz bil-habl	skipping
قَفَص	qafas	cage
قلعة	qal 'a	castle
قَلعة رَملية	qala'a ramliya	sandcastle
قَلَم حِبر	qalam hibr	pen
قلم رصاص	qalam rasaas	pencil
قَليل	qaleel	few
قَمَر	qamar	moon
قَميص	qamees	shirt, sweatshirt, t-shirt
قَميص داخلي	qamees daakhilee	vest
قَميص نوم	qamees nawm	nightdress
قُن دَجاج	qun dajaaj	hen house
قَناة	qanaa	canal
قُنَّبيط	qunnabeet	cauliflower
قُنفُذ	qunfuth	hedgehog
قَهوة	qahwa	coffee
قوس قُزَح	qaws quzah	rainbow

ك

كَبير	kabeer	big
كِتابة	kitaaba	writing
كُتُب	kutub	books
كَثير	katheer	many
كَراتي	karaatee	karate
كُراث	kuraath	leek
كُرة	kura	ball
كُرة أرضية	kura ardiyya	globe
كُرة الريشة	kurat ur-reesha	badminton
كُرة السَلّة	kurat us-salla	basketball
كُرة الطاولة	kurat ut-taawila	table tennis
كُرة القاعدة	kurat ul-qaa'ida	baseball
كُرة القَدَم	kurat ul-qadam	football
كُرة المضرب	kurat ul-madrib	tennis
كُرة قَدَم أمريكية	kurat qadam amreekiya	American football
كَرَز	karaz	cherry
كُرسي	kursee	chair, stool
كُرسي متحرك	kursee mutaharrek	wheelchair
كُرسي مَركَب	kursee markab	deck chair
كَرَفس	karafs	celery
كَركَدَن	karkadan	rhinoceros
كريكِت	kreekit	cricket
كَسر	kasr	breaking
كَعكة	ka'ka	cake
كَعكة عيد ميلاد	ka'kat 'eed meelaad	birthday cake
كُفوف	kufoof	paws
كَلب	kalb	dog

كَلب الراعي	kalb ur-raa'ee	sheepdog
كَنار	kanar	canary
كَنزة صوف	kanzat soof	jumper
كَنس	kans	sweeping
كنغر	kangar	kangaroo
كوع	koo'	elbow
كوكَب	kawkab	planet

ل

لِباس نوم	libaas nawm	pyjamas
لَبَن رائب	laban raa'ib	yoghurt
لحاف	lihaaf	duvet
لَحّام	lahhaam	butcher
لَحم	lahm	meat
لِسان	lisaan	tongue
لَعِب	la'ib	playing
لُعبة تركيبيّة	lu'ba tarkeebiyya	jigsaw
لوح	lawh	board
لوح أسوَد	lawh aswad	easel
لَوح تَزلّج	lawh tazalluj	snowboarding
لوح خَشَب	lawh khashab	plank
لوح شراعي	lawh shiraa'ee	windsurfing
لَوحة تَزلّج	lawhat tazalluj	skateboard,
ليفة	leefah	sponge
لَيل	layl	night
ليمون	laymoon	lemon

م

مُؤخّرة	mu'akhira	bottom
ماء	maa'	water
ماعِز	maa'iz	goat
مَبرَد	mabrad	file
مُبَلّل	muballal	wet
مَتبَنة	matbana	haystack
مِتر	mitr	tape measure
اَلمِثقَب	al-mithqab	drill
مُثَلَّث	muthalath	triangle
مِجداف	mijdaaf	oar, paddle
مِجرَفة	mijrafa	spade, hoe
مَجرود	majrood	dustpan
مَجلّة فُكاهية	majalla fukahiyya	comic
مِحدَلة	mihdala	roller
مِحراث	mihraalh	plough
مُحَرّك	muharrik	engine
مَحَطّة القطار	mahattat ul-qitaar	railway station
محفظة	mihfaza	purse
مَحقَنة	mihqana	syringe
مَخَدّة	mikhaddah	cushion
مَخروط	makhroot	cone
مَخزن	makhzan	shed
مَخزَن القَمح	makhzan ul-qamh	hayloft
مُخفّف صَدمات	mukhaffif sadamaat	buffers
مَدخَل	madkhal	hall
مَدخَنة	madkhana	chimney
مُدَرَّج	mudarraj	runway
مَدرَسة	madrasa	school
المَدرَسة	al-madrasa	the school
مَدينة المَلاهي	madeenat al-malaahee	fairground
مذياع	mizyaa'	radio
اَلمِرآب	al-mir'aab	garage
مِرآة	mir'aa	mirror
مُرَبَّع	muraba'	square
مُرَبّى	murabbaa	jam
مُرتَفِع	murtafi'	high
مِرحاض	mirhaad	toilet
مِرش	mirash	watering can
مَرشّة	mirashah	shower
مَرطَبانات	martabaanaat	jars
مركب بَضائع	markib badaa'i'	barge
مركَب شراعي	markib shiraa'ee	boat, sailing boat
مَرمى	marma	target
مَرنَب	marnab	guinea pig
مُرَوّض	murawwid	ringmaster
مُرَوّضة الجياد	murawwidat ul-jiyaad	bareback rider
مريح	mureeh	soft, comfortable
مريلة	miryala	apron
مُزارع	muzaari'	farmer
مَزالِج	mazaalij	ski, ice skates
مَزرعة	mazra'a	farmhouse
المَزرَعة	al-mazra'a	farm
مزمار	mizmaar	recorder
مَساء	masaa'	evening
مَسامير	masaameer	nails
مَسامير رَسم	masaameer rasm	tacks
مَسبَح	masbah	swimming pool
المُستشفى	al-mustashfaa	hospital
مُستَطيل	mustateel	rectangle
مَسحوق غَسيل	mashooq ghaseel	washing powder
مسطَرة	mistara	ruler
مَسطَرين	mastareen	trowel
مُشاهَدة	mushaahada	watching
مشط	misht	comb
مِشط زراعي	misht zira'ee	rake
مشمش	mishmish	apricot
مَشي	mashee	walking
مُصارعة سومو	musaara'at soomo	sumo wrestling
مصاصة الشرب	massasat ush-shurb	straw
مصباح	misbaah	lightbulb
مصباح	misbaah	lamp
مصعد	mis'ad	lift
مَصنع	masna'	factory
مُصوّر	musawwir	photographer
مَضَخّة البنزين	madakhat al-banzeen	petrol pump
مضرَب	madrab	bat, racket
مُضيء	mudee'	light
اَلمَطار	al-mataar	airport
اَلمَطبَخ	al-matbakh	kitchen
مَطَر	matar	rain
مطرَقة	mitraqa	hammer
مطواة	matwaa	penknife
مظلّة	mithalla	parachute, umbrella
مُظلم	muthlim	dark
معجون أسنان	ma'joon asnaan	toothpaste
معطَف	mi'taf	coat
مَعكَرونة	ma'karoona	spaghetti
مُعلّبات	mu'allabaat	tins
مَعين	ma'een	diamond
مَغسل سيارات	maghsal sayyaarat	car wash
مَغسَلة	maghsala	basin
مغطس	maghtas	bath
مُغلَق	mughlaq	closed
مُغنية	mughaniya	singers
مفتاح	miftaah	key, spanner
مفتاح الكَهرَباء	miftaah ul-kahrabaa'	switch
مفتش تذاكر	mufattish tathaakir	ticket inspector
مَفتوح	maftouh	open
مفَك	mifak	screwdriver
مَقبض الباب	mikbad-ul-bab	door handle
مَقَصّ	miqass	scissors
مِقَص الحَشيش	miqass ul-hasheesh	lawnmower
مَقطورة	maqtoora	carriages
مَقعَد	maq'ad	bench

مقعَد هَوائي	maq'ad hawaa'ee	chairlift
مِقلاة	miqlaa	frying pan
مَقهى	maqhaa	café
مَكتَب	maktab	desk
مُكعَّب	muka"ab	cube
مُكعَّبات	muka'abaat	bricks
مكنسة	miknasa	broom
مِكنسة كَهرَبائية	miknasa kahrabaa'iya	vacuum cleaner
مكواة	mikwaa	iron
مَلابِس السباحة	malaabis us-sibaaha	swimsuit
مَلابِسي	malaabis	my clothes
مَلاعِق خَشَب	malaa'iq khashab	spoons
مَلاعِق صغيرة	malaa'iq sagheera	teaspoons
ملح	milh	salt
مَلزَمة	malzama	vice
مُلصَقات	mulsaqaat	pictures
مَلعب	mal'ab	playgroond
مَلفوف	malfoof	cabbage
مَليء	malee'	full
مُمَثِّل	mumathil	actor
مُمَثِّلة	mumathila	actress
ممحاة	mimhaa	rubber
مَمَر	mamarr	path
مَمَر مُشاة	mamarr mushaa	crossing
مُمَرِّض	mumarrid	nurse
ممسَحة	mimsaha	duster
ممسَحة بعَصا	mimsaha bi'asaa	mop
مَناديل وَرَق	manaadeel waraq	tissues
مَنارة	manara	lighthouse
مُنخفِض	munkhafid	low
منديل	mindeel	handkerchief
المَنزل	al-manzil	the home
منشار	minshaar	saw
مَنشَفة	minshafa	towel
مَنطاد	mintaad	hot-air balloon
مَنظار	minthaar	telescope
منقار	minqaar	beak
مُهَرِّج	muharrij	clown
موز	mawz	banana
مَيِّت	mayyit	dead
ميزان	meezaan	seesaw
ميزان	meezaan	scales
ميزان حَرارة	meezaan haraara	thermometer
ميكانيكي	meekaaneekee	mechanic - man
ميكانيكية	meekaaneekiya	mechanic - woman

ن

نادِل	naadil	waiter
نادِلة	naadila	waitress
نار	naar	bonfire
الناس	an-naas	people
نافذة	naafitha	window
ناقِلة نَفط	naaqilat naft	oil tanker
نَبتة	nabta	plant
نَجار	najjaar	carpenter

نِجارة	nijaara	shavings
نَجمة	najma	star
نَجمةالبَحر	najmat ul-bahr	starfish
نَحلة	nahla	bee
نَحيف	naheef	thin
نَدى	nadaa	dew
نُزهة	nuzha	picnic
نسيج عنكبوت	naseej 'ankaboot	cobweb
نشارة	nishaara	sawdust
نَظارات	nathaaraat	glasses
نظيف	natheef	clean
نعال	ni'aal	slippers
نَعامة	na'aama	ostrich
نَفخ	nafkh	blowing
نَفق	nafaq	tunnel
نَقانِق	naqaaniq	sausage
نقود	nuqood	money
نَمِر	namir	tiger
نَهار	nahaar	morning
نَهر	nahr	river
نورَس	nawras	seagull
نوم	nawm	sleeping

ه

هاتف	haatif	telephone
هارمونيكا	harmoonikaa	mouth organ
هَدايا	hadaaya	presents
هَدية	hadiya	present
هرة	hirra	cat
هُرَيرة	hurayira	kitten
هلال	hilaal	crescent
همستر	hamster	hamster

و

واحد	waahid	one
واقي شَمسي	waaqee shamsee	suncream
وَجه	wajh	face
وَحل	wahl	mud
وراء	wara'	back
وَردي	wardi	pink
الوَرشة	al-warsha	workshop
وَرَق	waraq	paper
وَرَق حمام	waraq hammam	toilet paper
وَرَق زُجاج	waraq zujaaj	sandpaper
ورق زينة	waraq zeena	paper chains
وسادة	wisaada	pillow
وِسخ	wasikh	dirty
وَصيفة	waseefa	bridesmaid
وَلَد	walad	boy

ي

يَد	yad	hand
يَسار	yasaar	left
يَمين	yameen	right
يوسفي	yusufee	clementine
يوم الزَّفاف	yawm uz-zafaaf	wedding day